### Super-Duper Series

# Terrific Transportation!

by Annalisa McMorrow
illustrated by Marilynn G. Barr

Publisher: Roberta Suid
Design & Production: Scott McMorrow
Cover Design: David Hale
Cover Art: Mike Artell

Also in the Super-Duper series:
*Incredible Insects!* (MM 2018), *Spectacular Space!* (MM 2019), *Outstanding Oceans!* (MM 2020), *Wacky Weather!* (MM 2057), *Peculiar Plants!* (MM 2058), *Amazing Animals!* (MM 2059), *Leapin' Lizards!* (MM 2100), *Exciting Earth!* (MM 2101), and *Marvelous Money!* (MM 2103)

Entire contents copyright © 2000 by
Monday Morning Books, Inc.
For a complete catalog, please write to the address below:

P.O. Box 1680
Palo Alto, CA 94302

E-mail us at: MMBooks@aol.com
Visit our Web site: www.mondaymorningbooks.com
Call us at: 1-800-255-6049

Monday Morning is a registered trademark of
Monday Morning Books, Inc.

Permission is hereby granted to reproduce student materials
in this book for non-commercial individual or classroom use.

ISBN 1-57612-112-7

Printed in the United States of America
987654321

# Contents

| | |
|---|---|
| Introduction | 4 |
| All About Transportation | 6 |

### Hands-On Discoveries
| | |
|---|---|
| Early Boats | 8 |
| How Vehicles Are Named | 9 |
| Best Bumper Stickers | 11 |
| License Plate Lingo | 12 |
| Message on a Blimp | 13 |
| Artsy Automobiles | 15 |
| Super Sign Language | 17 |
| Caboose Keepsake Boxes | 19 |
| Watching the Road | 20 |
| As Quick as a Kangaroo | 22 |
| Seat Belts Save Lives! | 24 |
| Super-Duper Project: | |
| Create-a-Car | 25 |

### Nonfiction Book Links
| | |
|---|---|
| Interview with a Vehicle | 26 |
| Learning About Lighthouses | 29 |
| Hot Air Balloon Reports | 32 |
| Across the Prairie | 34 |
| Trip on the *Titanic* | 36 |
| Vehicle ABC Book | 38 |
| Four-Part Reports | 39 |
| Vehicle Glossaries | 41 |
| "All Aboard!" Spelling Bee | 43 |
| Super-Duper Project: | |
| Traffic Jam Mural | 47 |

### Fiction Book Links
| | |
|---|---|
| *The Boxcar Children* | 49 |
| Write It on a Box Car | 50 |
| *Little House on the Prairie* | 52 |
| Little House Diary | 53 |
| *The Magic School Bus* | 55 |
| The Magic Trailer | 57 |
| *Chitty-Chitty-Bang-Bang* | 58 |
| Chitty-Chitty for Sale | 59 |
| Super-Duper Project: | |
| Making Mother Goose Rhymes | 60 |

### It's Show Time!
| | |
|---|---|
| Terrific Transportation Program | 62 |
| Would You Drive Real Far? | 63 |
| Cardboard Car Costume | 64 |
| A Hovercraft Glides on the Ocean | 65 |
| Submarine, Submarine | 65 |
| Super Submarine Costume | 66 |
| Oh, Give Me a Boat | 67 |
| Oh, My Darling, Submarine | 68 |
| Hovercrafts, Submarines... | 69 |

### Resources
| | |
|---|---|
| Super-Duper Fact Cards | 70 |
| Transportation A to Z List | 78 |
| Transportation Resources | 79 |

# Introduction: Why Transportation?

Planes, trains, and automobiles fascinate most children. With the activities in this book, your students will learn about the exciting world of transportation, while practicing writing, reading, math, research, performance, and speaking skills. They'll interview a vehicle and much more. Most of the activities in this book can be simplified for younger students or extended for upper grades.

*Terrific Transportation!* is divided into four parts and a resource section. Through a variety of activities, **Hands-On Discoveries** will help answer questions such as "How are vehicles named?" and "What did early boats look like?" Reproducible sheets with a special car icon have directions written specifically for the children.

**Nonfiction Book Links** feature speaking, writing, and reporting activities based on nonfiction resources. Many activities are accompanied by helpful handouts, which will lead the children through the research procedure. When research is required, you have the option of letting children look for the facts needed in your classroom, school, local library, or on the Internet. Or use the "Super-Duper Fact Cards" located in the resource section at the back of this book. These cards list information for 16 transportation-related subjects. You can duplicate the cards onto neon-colored paper, laminate, and cut them out. Then store the cards in a box for children to choose from when doing their research. These cards also provide an opportunity for younger children to participate in research projects. The research is provided for them on easy-to-read cards.

*Terrific Transportation* © 2000 Monday Morning Books, Inc.

The **Fiction Book Links** section uses chapter books and storybooks to introduce information about transportation. This section's activities, projects, and language extensions help children see connections between vehicles and the world around them. Each "Link" also includes a tongue twister. You can challenge children to create their own twisters from the transportation facts and words they've learned. Also included in this section are decorating suggestions (called "setting the stage") for each particular book. Creating a book-friendly environment in the classroom will encourage children to read on their own for fun.

**It's Show Time!** presents new songs sung to old tunes. The songs can be duplicated and given to the children to learn. If you want to hold a performance, write each performer's name on the reproducible program page and distribute the copies to your audience. Consider having the children make costumes to go with the songs. (Both costumes require a bit of adult help. For the car and submarine costume, cut the top and bottom off each box and poke four holes in each box, two in front and two in back, before giving the boxes to the children to paint.)

Three sections in this book end with a "Super-Duper Project," an activity that uses the information children have learned in the unit. A choral performance is one possible "Super-Duper" ending for the "It's Show Time!" section.

# All About Transportation

Before there were cars, people got around on foot. Later, they rode in horsedrawn wagons and carriages. The inventors of automobiles had to invent a carriage that would turn its own wheels. In the first cars, the driver had to turn a handle on the front of a car to get it started. Now, all drivers have to do is turn a key. Today's cars have many safety features that were missing from horsedrawn carriages. These include headlights, taillights, windshield wipers, and horns. Cars continue to change. In the future, cars may be run by solar power or on electric batteries.

Since the invention of the car, people have created many different unusual vehicles. The German Amphicar (created in the 1960s) could travel on water or land. The Aerocar was a flying car made to avoid traffic jams. A fruit company created "mobile oranges" that were round, fruit-shaped automobiles.

# All About Transportation

There are many different types of buses —school buses, city buses, extra-long buses, double-decker buses, and tour buses. The first buses, which started service in Paris in 1662, were actually pulled by horses!

Trains do an assortment of jobs. Freight trains carry objects and passenger trains carry people. Some trains travel underground. These trains are called subways or metros. Trains that travel above the streets are called elevated trains. Trains travel along tracks. Most trains travel on two tracks, but monorails travel on single tracks.

Some planes have jet engines. Others use propellers. Some airplanes are large and carry many passengers. Others carry only freight or cargo. Some planes can actually land on water. These planes are called seaplanes. They have special landing devices that let them float. People who fly airplanes are called pilots.

HANDS-ON DISCOVERY

# Early Boats

Before boats, the first method of transportation that people used on water was probably a floating log or tree trunk. Later, people placed branches side by side and tied them together to make rafts. Eventually, paddles were added to help propel the rafts.

## Materials:
Craft sticks, water-proof glue, straws, clay, water source (water table or dish pan filled with water)

## Directions:
1. Have the children pretend they live 10,000 years BC. They have never seen a boat or a raft.
2. Provide craft sticks, glue, clay, and straws for the children to use to make their own miniature rafts.
3. Once the glue has dried, let the children test their rafts in the water. If the rafts don't float, the children can experiment again with new designs.
4. Post the completed rafts and boats on a table with boat-themed reading materials.

## Boat information to share with the children:
• Dugouts were the first real boats. They were made by hollowing out a split tree, either by burning out the wood, or gouging it out with stone tools.
• Quffas were round basket boats. These boats were used on the Euphrates River in Babylonia.
• Skin boats were used around 5000 BC. Animal skins were sewn together and stretched over a frame of branches or basketwork.

Terrific Transportation © 2000 Monday Morning Books, Inc.

HANDS-ON DISCOVERY

# How Vehicles Are Named

Vehicles have gotten their names many different ways. Some vehicles are named after their inventors, such as the railroad sleeping cars named after the designer George Pullman. Other vehicles are named to describe what they are made of, such as skin boats, which were made from animal skins. Other vehicles are named for their purpose, such as lifeboats, or their skill, such as the Wright Brothers' plane, the *Flyer*. Today, manufacturers give their vehicles names to differentiate them from similar vehicles.

**Materials:**
"Naming Vehicles" Hands-on Handout (p. 10), pens or pencils

**Directions:**
1. Duplicate a handout for each child.
2. Discuss the fact that vehicles have gotten their names in many different ways. If a child were to invent a new vehicle, it might be named after him or her!
3. Give each child a chance to name a vehicle by looking at the vehicles on the hands-on handout and coming up with new names for each one.
4. Once the children have finished filling out the sheet, let them share their ideas with the class.

**Book Link:**
• *Dorling Kindersley Visual Timeline of Transportation* by Anthony Wilson (Dorling Kindersley, 1995).

Terrific Transportation © 2000 Monday Morning Books, Inc.

# Naming Vehicles

Some vehicles were named after their inventors. Others were named to describe their functions. Many companies give their vehicles special names. Some car companies name their cars after animals, including Mustangs, Beetles, Rabbits, and Cougars.

Vehicles named after their inventors include:

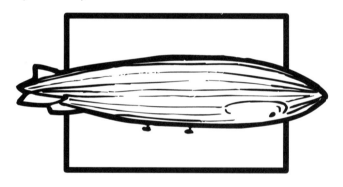

Ford motor cars (named for Henry Ford)

The Zeppelin, a type of airship, was named after Count Ferdinand von Zeppelin.

Harley-Davidson Motorcycles were named for their makers, William Harley and the three Davidson brothers.

Look at the vehicles above. Create a new name for each vehicle. You might choose an animal name or a name that describes the size, shape, or purpose of the vehicle.

*Terrific Transportation* © 2000 monday Morning Books, Inc.

HANDS-ON DISCOVERY

# Best Bumper Stickers

Bumper stickers are written for a variety of reasons. Some are simply funny. Others urge people to action, such as "Save Mono Lake."

**Materials:**
Construction paper, scissors, crayons or markers, scratch paper, pens or pencils

**Directions:**
1. Cut the construction paper into strips that are the size of bumper stickers. Make one per child.
2. Discuss bumper stickers with the students. Have them share their favorite bumper stickers.
3. Have the children write their own bumper stickers. They should start by using the scratch paper for brainstorming. Remind the students that bumper stickers have limited space. They should keep their messages short. The children can write bumper stickers that urge people to action, that proclaim their views on subjects, or that are funny or silly.
4. Once the children are happy with their statements, they can copy them over on the bumper sticker-sized construction paper.
5. Post the children's bumper stickers on a "Best Bumper Stickers" bulletin board.

**Options:**
• Have the children pay attention to bumper stickers they see. They can write down any that they like in a notebook to share with the class.
• Decals for cars come in different shapes and sizes. The children can cut their own shapes for their bumper stickers.

Terrific Transportation © 2000 Monday Morning Books, Inc.

# License Plate Lingo

Most license plates have no meaning. They are simply an assortment of letters and numbers. However, some drivers special-order plates called "vanity plates." These license plates have special meanings for the drivers.

**Materials:**
Construction paper, scissors, crayons or markers, scratch paper, pens or pencils

**Directions:**
1. Explain that the children will be creating license plates for their future cars. Discuss the topic of "vanity plates." Let the children share any that they might have seen.
2. Explain that when creating a "vanity plate" only a specific number of letters, numbers, and spaces can be used.
3. Have the children use the scratch paper to brainstorm plates that might work for them. They can use up to ten spaces.
4. Once the children are happy with their plates, they can copy the plates onto construction paper.
5. Post the completed license plates on a "License Plate Lingo" bulletin board. Viewers can try to decipher the different plates.

**Options:**
- Discuss using numbers as part of abbreviations. For example: gr8 = great, st8 = state, l8= late, pl8 = plate, 4 = for, 2 = to or too.
- Discuss letter abbreviations, such as: QT = cutie, MT = empty, LYF = life, R = our or are, N = and.

HANDS-ON DISCOVERY

# Message on a Blimp

Blimps often travel over sporting events, proclaiming messages on their electronic banners. Children may have seen blimps in the sky or on television. The necessary brevity of the messages on the blimps will make children more aware of editing their writing.

**Materials:**
Blimp Pattern (p. 14), crayons or markers, scratch paper, pens or pencils

**Directions:**
1. Discuss blimps. Have the children share any experiences they may have had, either seeing a blimp on television or in person. If any child has ridden in a blimp, let him or her share the experience.
2. Duplicate a copy of the Blimp Pattern for each child.
3. Have the children think of a message that they consider important for everyone in their school to know. Or have them brainstorm messages that they would like to share with their family.
4. Once the children write their messages on scratch paper, have them look at the length of the messages. Will their messages fit on the space of the blimp? If not, have them edit the messages to fit.
5. The children can write their messages in the space on the blimp pattern. Then they can color in the rest of the pattern or cut out the blimp so that it stands alone.
6. Either post the blimps in the classroom, or let the children take them home to hang in their rooms or on their doors.

**Option:**
• Use the blimps to get out the word about a school or class event—such as a play or musical (your vehicle-themed musical would be one event).

Terrific Transportation © 2000 Monday Morning Books, Inc.

HANDS-ON DISCOVERY

## Blimp Pattern

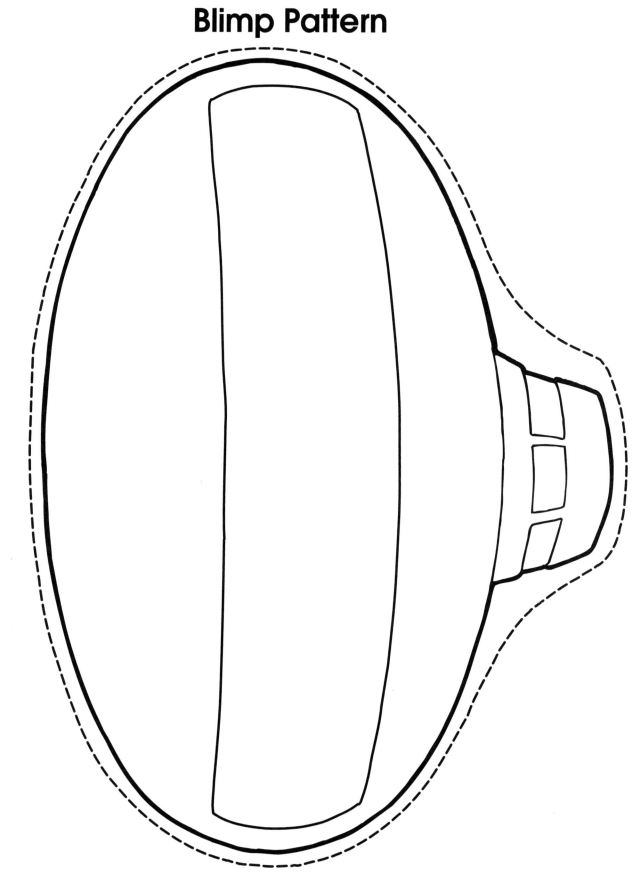

HANDS-ON DISCOVERY

# Artsy Automobiles

Some people take their cars very seriously. They wash them and care for them constantly. Others have more artistic relationships with their cars. They use their cars as a means to express themselves. Cars that have been decorated by the owners are called "art cars."

**Materials:**
Automobile Pattern (p. 16), crayons or markers, heavy paper, scissors, hole punch, yarn, glue, tempera paint, paintbrushes, shallow tins (for paint), sequins (other decorative items, such as buttons, glitter, lace or fabric scraps)

**Directions:**
1. Discuss art cars. Have the children share any experiences they may have had, either seeing an art car in person or on television.
2. Duplicate a copy of the Automobile Pattern onto heavy paper for each child.
3. Have the children brainstorm how they would like to decorate their cars.
4. Provide a wide assortment of items for the children to use to turn their Automobile Patterns into art cars.
5. Once the cars have dried, post them in a parade around the classroom.

**Book Link:**
• *Wild Wheels* by Harrold Blank (Pomegranate Artbooks, 1994).
This book includes pictures of many different art cars, plus stories about the owners. Choose which pictures and stories you would like to share with the children.

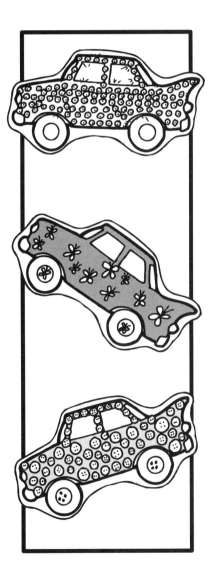

Terrific Transportation © 2000 Monday Morning Books, Inc.

HANDS-ON DISCOVERY

# Automobile Pattern

*Terrific Transportation* © 2000 Monday Morning Books, Inc.

HANDS-ON DISCOVERY

# Super Sign Language

Public signs must be understood by people who may not share the same language. Some signs that are necessary in one country wouldn't make sense in another. For instance, in Australia, kangaroo crossing signs are common. Those would seem out of place anywhere in the United States.

**Materials:**
Public Sign Page (p. 18), paper, crayons and markers

**Directions:**
1. Duplicate a copy of the Public Sign Page for each child.
2. Working together as a class, have the children decipher the meanings of each symbol.
3. Have the children try to think of symbols that are missing from these public signs.
4. Provide crayons and markers for the children to use to make their own public signs. The signs should be able to be understood by people who don't speak English.
5. Post the completed Public Signs in the classroom.

**Options:**
• Have the children create signs that are needed in your school. For instance, signs could represent "No talking" for the library, "Clean your table" for the lunch area, "No running" for hallways, and so on.
• This would be an appropriate time to discuss signs that children should pay attention to, such as railroad crossing signs, stop signs, and walk/don't walk signs.

Terrific Transportation © 2000 Monday Morning Books, Inc.

 HANDS-ON HANDOUT

# Public Sign Page

HANDS-ON DISCOVERY

# Caboose Keepsake Boxes

In this activity, children will create their own shoe box train cars. The train boxes can be used for decoration, or children can use them for keepsake storage.

**Materials:**
Shoe boxes with lids (one per child), tempera paint, shallow tins for paint, construction paper, scissors, glue, books about trains (see **Transportation Resources**)

**Directions:**
1. Show the children pictures of trains in books.
2. Give each child a shoe box and explain that the children will be making their own train cars. They can make cabooses, engines, freight cars, or passenger cars.
3. Provide a variety of art materials for the children to use to decorate the boxes.
4. Once the boxes are dry, the children can take them home.

**Option:**
• Save the train boxes for decorating the room for *The Boxcar Children* activity (p. 49).

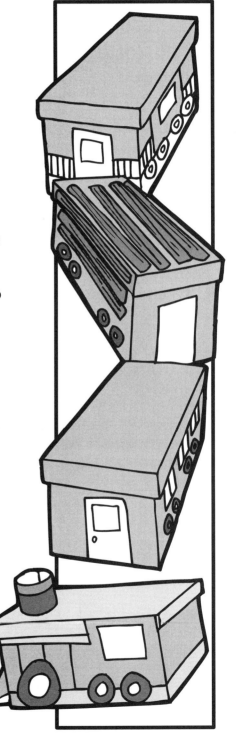

Terrific Transportation © 2000 Monday Morning Books, Inc.

# Watching the Road

This cooperative graphing homework activity lets the entire class work together. Have the children estimate ahead of time how many of each vehicle they think they'll see—or which vehicle will be the most common. Once the graph is completed, see if the children were right.

## Materials:
"Traffic Chart" Hands-on Handout (p. 21), chalkboard and colored chalk or large sheet of paper and colored pens

## Directions:
1. Duplicate a copy of the "Traffic Chart" for each child.
2. Have the children spend a weekend keeping track of how many of each vehicle they see. If children see vehicles that aren't on the chart, they can write the names of the vehicles on the back of the paper.
3. When the children bring their charts back to the classroom, have them tally up the number of check marks by each vehicle.
4. Work as a class to make a bar graph of the vehicles. Write the names of the vehicles on the bottom of the page (or chalkboard), and write numbers along the left-hand side. Have the children help fill in the graph by adding the numbers of vehicles they each charted.
5. Read the graph as a class to discover which vehicles rule the road!

HANDS-ON HANDOUT

# Traffic Chart

Make a check mark next to each vehicle that you see. On the back of this page, keep track of vehicles that aren't on the chart.

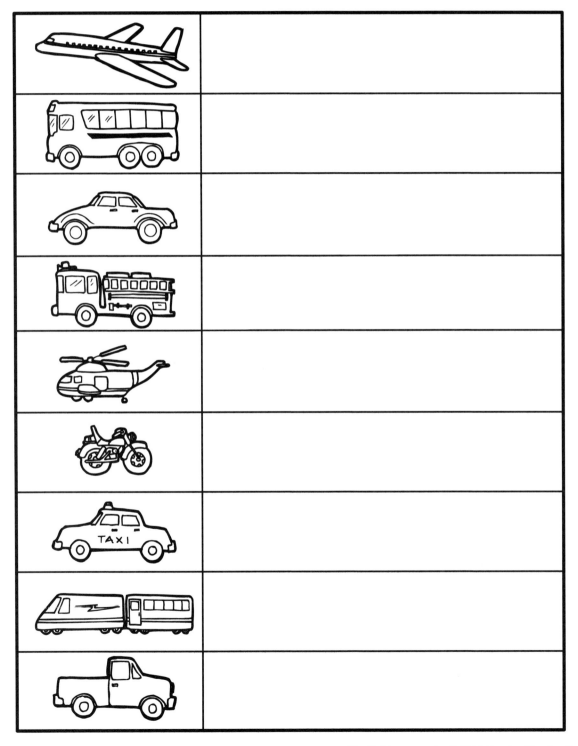

Terrific Transportation © 2000 Monday Morning Books, Inc.

HANDS-ON DISCOVERY

# As Quick as a Kangaroo

## Materials:
"Kangaroo Road Map" Hands-on Handout (p. 23), paper, pencils, rulers, calculators (optional)

## Directions:
1. Explain that kangaroos can travel up to 40 miles (64 km) per hour.
2. Duplicate a copy of the "Kangaroo Road Map" handout for each child or each pair of children.
3. Have the children look at the distances between cities on the map. Then have them figure out how long it would take a kangaroo traveling at 40 miles (64 km) per hour to make the journeys. Children can use calculators to do these problems or work together in small groups to solve the problems. Demonstrate how to do the division to figure out the answers.
4. Explain that in 1865, British law limited self-propelled (not horse-driven) road vehicles to 4 mph (6 kph). Have the children figure out how long it would have taken these vehicles to travel the same distances. (The kangaroo travels ten times faster!)

## Option:
• Have the children use maps or atlases to find the distances between their town and the next town or between different famous towns. Ask the children to figure out how long it would take a kangaroo, or a self-propelled vehicle in 1865, to make the journeys.

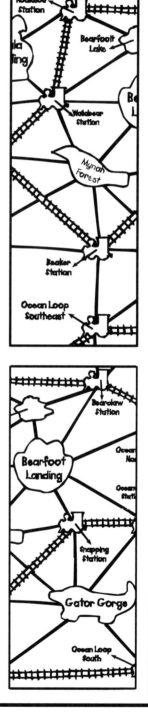

Terrific Transportation © 2000 Monday Morning Books, Inc.

HANDS-ON HANDOUT

# Kangaroo Road Map

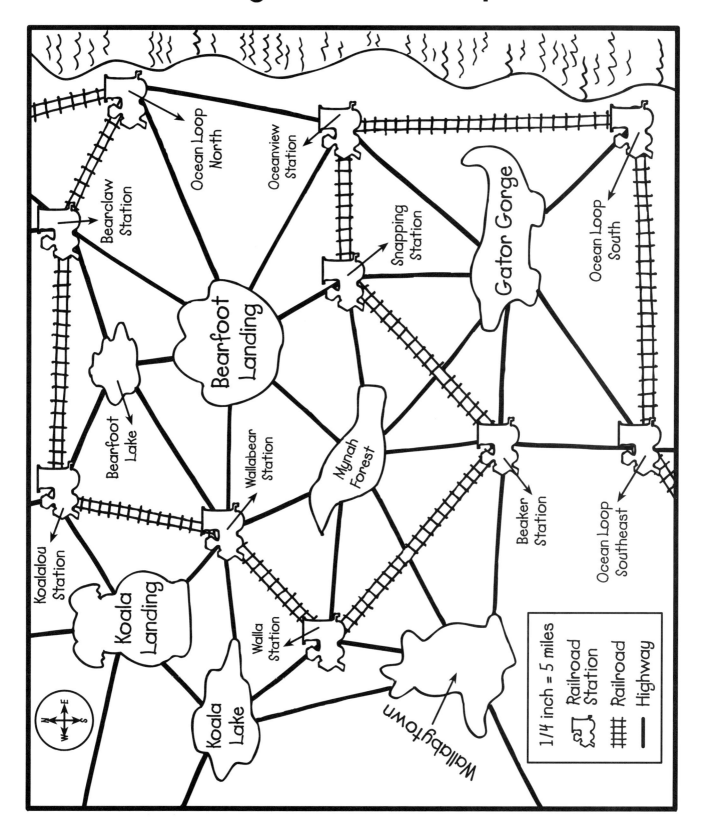

*Terrific Transportation* © 2000 Monday Morning Books, Inc.

HANDS-ON DISCOVERY

# Seat Belts Save Lives!

In many states, seat belts are required by law. However, some people continue to forget to wear their seat belts.

## Materials:
Drawing paper, crayons or markers, pens or pencils

## Directions:
1. Discuss passenger safety and the concept of wearing seat belts.
2. Explain that the children will be brainstorming slogans to remind people to buckle up.
3. Divide the children into teams of two or four. Have the teams work together to come up with seat belt slogans.
4. Once the teams decide on a slogan, they should illustrate it on a large piece of paper.
5. Use the seat belt slogans in a safety campaign for your school. Post the pictures in the library, lunch room, or multipurpose room where many classes can see them.

## Option:
• Use this activity to create slogans and pictures for other forms of safety awareness, such as stopping at stop signs, wearing bicycle helmets, and not talking to strangers.

Terrific Transportation © 2000 Monday Morning Books, Inc.

HANDS-ON DISCOVERY: SUPER-DUPER PROJECT

# Create-a-Car

Once the children have learned about a wide variety of vehicles, they can create their own from assorted scraps, recyclables, boxes, and found objects.

## Materials:
All About Transportation (pp. 6-7), recyclables (cardboard boxes, paper bags, toilet roll and paper towel tubes, lids, cartons), fabric and yarn scraps, glue, paste, construction paper, glitter mixed with glue (in squeeze bottles), buttons, sequins, tempera paint, paintbrushes, shallow tins (for paint), clay or playdough, crayons or markers, blue construction paper, clothesline

## Directions:
1. Duplicate the All About Transportation handouts for each child to read.
2. Provide a variety of materials for the children to use to create their own cars, planes, boats, trains, or other vehicles.
3. Once the creations are completed, let the children help you set up an in-class display:
• Hang flying vehicles from clothesline strung across the classroom.
• Cars, trucks, and buses can travel along roads set up on shelves, desks, and window sills.
• Display boats against blue construction paper backgrounds to represent the ocean.
4. Invite other classes or parents to observe the creative display.

## Option:
• Drivers of early automobiles wore an assortment of odd equipment, such as goggles and special hats. Have the children design clothing to be worn in their vehicles.

Terrific Transportation © 2000 Monday Morning Books, Inc.

NONFICTION BOOK LINKS

# Interview with a Vehicle

### Materials:
"Vehicle Fact Sheet" Hands-on Handout (p. 27), "Vehicle Interview Sheet" Hands-on Handout (p. 28), pencils or pens, "Super-Duper Fact Cards" (pp. 70-77)

### Directions:
1. Have the children each choose a form of transportation to research. Explain that the children will be pretending to be the form of transportation they are researching.
2. Duplicate one copy of the "Vehicle Fact Sheet" handout and the "Interview Sheet" for each child.
3. Have the children research the vehicles using the guidelines on the "Vehicle Interview Sheet" handout. They can use the "Super-Duper Fact Cards" at the end of the book, or they can use books from the library.
4. Once the children finish their research, divide them into pairs. Let each partner take a turn interviewing the other in front of the class.
5. Set up an interview schedule, perhaps working through five to six interviews per day.

### Option:
• Children can dress up to look like their chosen vehicles. They can make costumes from cardboard boxes and sheets.

### Note:
Children might choose to research people who were important to the world of transportation today, for example, the Wright brothers, Amelia Earhart, Henry Ford, Chuck Yeager, and so on.

Terrific Transportation © 2000 Monday Morning Books, Inc.

HANDS-ON HANDOUT

# Vehicle Fact Sheet

Use this fact sheet to record at least four facts about your chosen vehicle. (Remember to list the books you used. If you use fact cards, write "fact card" under "Books I used.") You can use the back of this sheet if you need more space.

My name is: _____

My vehicle is: _____

Fact: _____

Fact: _____

Fact: _____

Fact: _____

Books I used:

Title: _____

Author: _____

Title: _____

Author: _____

*Terrific Transportation* © 2000 Monday Morning Books, Inc.

HANDS-ON HANDOUT

# Vehicle Interview Sheet

Write your answers under the questions. Write your own question for question 5. Or use a new sheet of paper to write and answer all of your own questions. Your partner will use these questions to interview you in front of the class.

Question 1: What type of vehicle are you?
_____

Question 2: When were you invented?
_____

Question 3: How do you work?
_____

Question 4: What are you made of?
_____

Question 5:
_____
_____
_____
_____
_____
_____
_____

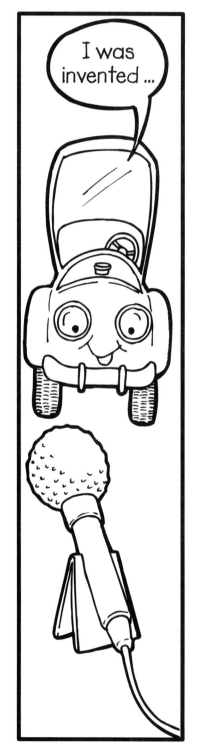

Terrific Transportation © 2000 Monday Morning Books, Inc.

NONFICTION BOOK LINKS

# Learning About Lighthouses

In this activity, the children can choose whether to study boats or lighthouses. The reports will be posted together in a cooperative mural.

**Materials:**
Lighthouse (p. 30), Boats (p. 31), "Super-Duper Fact Cards" on boats and lighthouses (pp. 71 and 74), crayons or markers, pens or pencils, tempera paints, paintbrushes, tins (for paint), books on boats and lighthouses

**Directions:**
1. Explain that the children will be writing miniature reports about boats or lighthouses. The children can choose which subject to research.
2. Provide books, "Super-Duper Fact Cards," encyclopedias, and any other resources for the children to use to do their research.
3. Duplicate the Lighthouse and Boat patterns for the children to use to write their reports.
4. Spread a large sheet of butcher paper on a flat surface. Have the children paint a sea-scene onto the paper.
5. When the painting dries, have the children post their reports directly onto the mural. They can glue boats in the water and post lighthouses on islands or cliffs.

**Options:**
• Assign different children to the different topics—a certain amount to lighthouses and a certain amount to boats.
• This activity could be done with airplanes and control towers. Each child could write a report on airplane-shaped pieces of paper. Post the reports around a control tower.

Terrific Transportation © 2000 Monday Morning Books, Inc.

NONFICTION BOOK LINKS

# Lighthouse

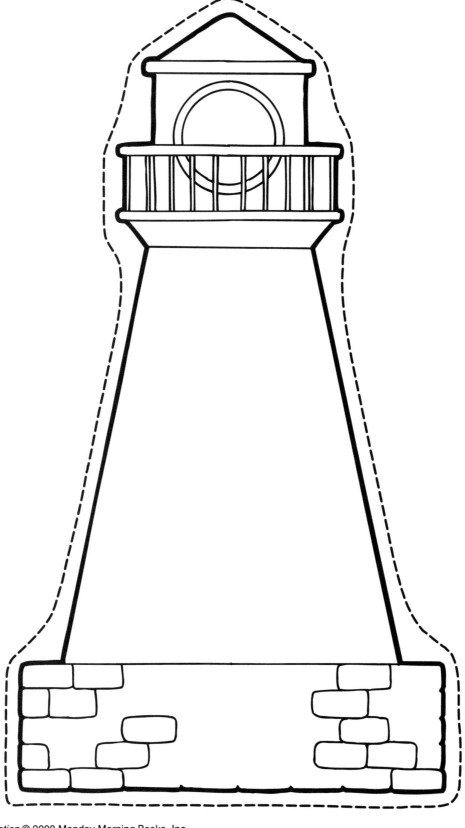

Terrific Transportation © 2000 Monday Morning Books, Inc.

# Boats

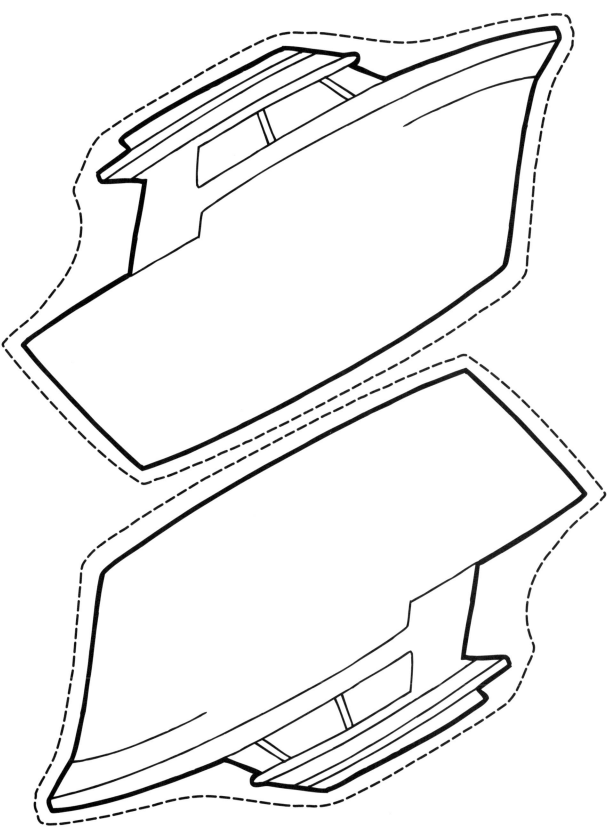

# Hot Air Balloon Reports

Hot air balloons create pretty pictures as they float in the sky. Your students' reports will look just as fetching posted around the classroom.

## Materials:
Hot Air Balloon (p. 33), "Super-Duper Fact Card" on hot air balloons (p. 73), scissors, pens or pencils, crayons or markers, sequins, glitter, glue

## Directions:
1. Duplicate a copy of the Hot Air Balloon for each child.
2. Have the children research hot air balloons using the "Super-Duper Fact Card," the Web, or other resources.
3. Have the children write their favorite facts on the baskets of the balloons.
4. Provide an assortment of crayons, markers, glitter, glue, sequins, and other art materials for the children to use to decorate the hot air balloons.
5. Post the completed balloons all around the classroom. The balloons should be at varying heights, but low enough so that visitors can read the facts written on the baskets.

## Options:
• The children can cut clouds from white construction paper to post around the balloons.
• Take the children on a field trip to watch real hot air balloons take off or land.
• Bring an assortment of colorful helium-filled balloons into the classroom as decoration for this activity.

NONFICTION BOOK LINKS

## Hot Air Balloon

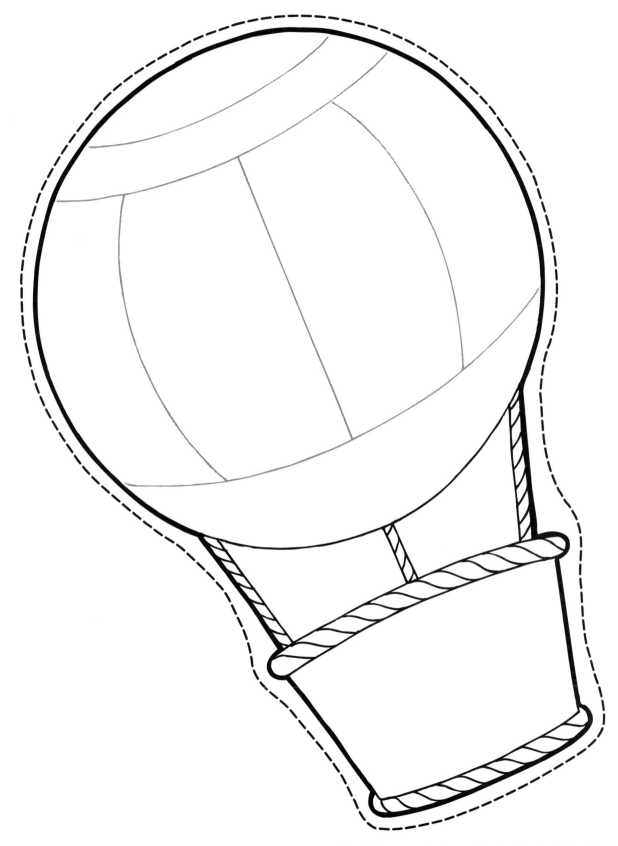

*Terrific Transportation* © 2000 Monday Morning Books, Inc.

NONFICTION BOOK LINKS

# Across the Prairie

Consider reading a related book, such as *Grandma Essie's Covered Wagon* by David Williams (Knopf, 1993) or *Little House on the Prairie* by Laura Ingalls Wilder (Harper & Row, 1935), to the children before doing this activity.

## Materials:
Prairie Schooner (p. 35), "Super-Duper Fact Card" on covered wagons (p. 72), scissors, pens or pencils, crayons or markers

## Directions:
1. Duplicate a copy of the Prairie Schooner for each child.
2. Have the children research covered wagons using the "Super-Duper Fact Card," the Web, or other resources.
3. Have the children write their favorite facts on the front of the Prairie Schooner patterns.
4. Post the completed prairie schooner reports in a chain around the classroom.

## Options:
• Let the children create a mural background for their schooners. They can replicate the wide grasslands, or prairies, covered by the wagon trains.
• Use green and gold colored crepe paper to create grasslands around the schooners.
• Set out an assortment of prairie-themed books for the children to read or look through.
• Create math problems as tie-ins to this assignment. The wagons traveled about 20 miles (30 km) a day. The entire trip across country could take more than five months. Have the children figure out the distance of the journey.

Terrific Transportation © 2000 Monday Morning Books, Inc.

NONFICTION BOOK LINKS

# Prairie Schooner

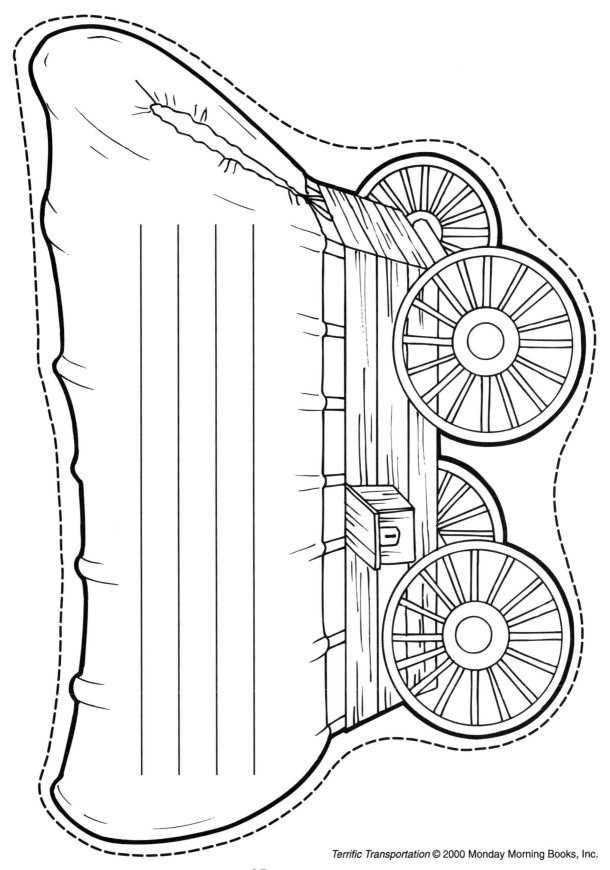

Terrific Transportation © 2000 Monday Morning Books, Inc.

35

NONFICTION BOOK LINKS

# Trip on the *Titanic*

In this activity, the children will pretend that they were passengers on the *Titanic*, and then write historical fiction pieces reporting on their experiences.

**Materials:**
*Titanic* Life Preserver (p. 37), "Super-Duper Fact Card" on The *Titanic* (p. 75), books about the *Titanic* (see **Transportation Resources**), scissors, pens or pencils

**Directions:**
1. Duplicate a copy of the *Titanic* Life Preserver for each child.
2. Explain that the children will be taking imaginary trips on the *Titanic*. After researching to find out facts about the *Titanic*, they will be writing brief reports as if they were passengers on the doomed ship.
3. The children can use the "Super-Duper Fact Card" on the *Titanic* for research. Or they can use encyclopedias, books, or the Web.
4. Once the children do their research, they should write brief reports on the lines in the center of the *Titanic* Life Preserver.
5. Post the completed preserver reports on a bulletin board in the library. Place *Titanic*-themed or other boat-related resources on a table below the reports.

**Option:**
• The children can write historical fiction reports based on other famous journeys, such as Marco Polo's trip to the Orient or Christopher Columbus' voyage to America.

*Terrific Transportation* © 2000 Monday Morning Books, Inc.

NONFICTION BOOK LINKS

# Titanic Life Preserver

# Vehicle ABC Book

In this assignment, children will work cooperatively to make a classroom ABC book. Share the book with other classes when it's finished, or donate it to your school library.

**Materials:**
Transportation A to Z List (p. 78), "Super-Duper Fact Cards" (p. 70-77), construction paper, crayons or markers, vehicle resources (see **Transportation Resources**), hole punch, yarn or brads

**Directions:**
1. Duplicate the Transportation A to Z list for the children to study.
2. Have each child choose one item on the list to research. The children can choose items that aren't on the list, but try to have at least one item for each letter of the alphabet.
3. Have the children research their vehicles, or vehicle-related topics, using the "Super-Duper Fact Cards," transportation-related resources, or the Web.
3. The children can illustrate their chosen topic and then write one or two sentences about it.
4. Bind the pages in a classroom Vehicle ABC book. Children can work together to make front and back covers.

**Note:**
If there aren't 26 children in your class, some children can research items for more than one letter. If there are more than 26 students, you can include more than one page per letter.

**Options:**
• Have each child write a short autobiography to include in an "about the authors" section at the back of the book. Show the children examples of brief biographies found at the backs of many books.
• Make other ABC books for different topics during the year.

Terrific Transportation © 2000 Monday Morning Books, Inc.

# Four-Part Reports

### Materials:
"Vehicle Reports" Hands-on Handout (p. 40), "Super-Duper Fact Cards" (pp. 70-77), pens or pencils

### Directions:
1. Divide the students into groups of four.
2. Have the children choose vehicle or transportation themes to research. They should choose subjects that have multiple parts, for example, a train (engine, passenger car, freight car, caboose), a car (engine, body, wheels, brakes), a boat (hull, rudder, sails, bow, stern), a motorcycle (handlebars, engine, wheels, throttle, brake). Once they've chosen a vehicle or theme, they should each choose one part to research.
3. Have the children brainstorm names for their groups, for example, "Marvelous Motorcycle," or "Terrific Train."
4. Each child in the group should learn two facts about his or her chosen part. They can either refer to the "Super-Duper Fact Cards" or do research using books in the library, encyclopedias, or the Web.
5. Have the children give reports to the class in their groups.

### Options:
• The children can create costumes to go with their chosen themes. They can wear the costumes when they present their reports.
• The children can write their reports on patterns from this book. For instance, children writing a report on trains could use the Train pattern (p. 46) and the Boxcar pattern (p. 51) and make their own missing patterns.

HANDS-ON HANDOUT

# Vehicle Reports

Name: _____

Date: _____

Name of group: _____

Theme of report: _____

Fact 1: _____

Fact 2: _____

Resources I used:

_____
_____
_____
_____
_____
_____

(Note: For books, list the title and the author.)

NONFICTION BOOK LINKS

# Vehicle Glossaries

### Materials:
"Vehicle Glossary" Hands-on Handout (p. 42), dictionaries, pencils, construction paper, stapler, crayons or markers

### Directions:
1. Duplicate one "Vehicle Glossary" Hands-on Handout for each child. Explain that a glossary is a list of special words with definitions listed after each word.
2. Have the children look up each word in the dictionary.
3. The children should write the definition next to the word to create their own vehicle glossaries. They can put the definitions into their own words. This will help them to remember the definitions later. Younger children can draw pictures to represent the meanings of the words.
4. As children learn new transportation words or phrases, they can add these to their glossaries.
5. Provide construction paper and a stapler for the children to use to bind their pages together. They can decorate the covers of the books with drawings of different transportation icons.

### Option:
White-out the words on the "Vehicle Glossary" handouts and duplicate one page for each child. Let the children write in their own transportation-related words and definitions.

Terrific Transportation © 2000 Monday Morning Books, Inc.

HANDS-ON HANDOUT

# Vehicle Glossary

| | |
|---|---|
| caravan | |
| pony express | |
| ski | |
| submarine | |
| taxi | |
| zeppelin | |

*Terrific Transportation* © 2000 Monday Morning Books, Inc.

NONFICTION BOOK LINKS

# "All Aboard!" Spelling Bee

**Materials:**
Ticket Word Patterns (pp. 44-45), Train (p. 46), crayons or markers, hat, scissors

**Directions:**
1. Duplicate the Ticket Word Patterns, making one copy for each child and a few extra sheets for teacher use.
2. Color the Train pattern and post it on a bulletin board. Cut out one extra set of tickets and post them around the train. (Cover the board before the spelling bee.)
3. Have the children learn how to spell each word. (You might give the children the sheets to take home and study at the beginning of the week, then have the spelling bee at the end of the week.)
4. Host a spelling bee in your classroom. Keep one set of tickets in a hat and pull out one at a time, asking each chid in turn to spell the word on the ticket. (Older children may be able to give you both the spelling and the definition of the word.)
5. Continue with the spelling bee, having each child who misspells a word sit down.

**Note:**
Choose words that are appropriate to your children's spelling level. If a word is difficult for the students, it could be classified as a bonus term. A child who misspells it won't have to sit down, but would get another turn with a different word.

**Options:**
• Duplicate blank tickets and let children write in their own transportation-related terms.
• Younger children can simply tape the tickets to sheets of writing paper and practice copying the words.

Terrific Transportation © 2000 Monday Morning Books, Inc.

# Ticket Word Patterns

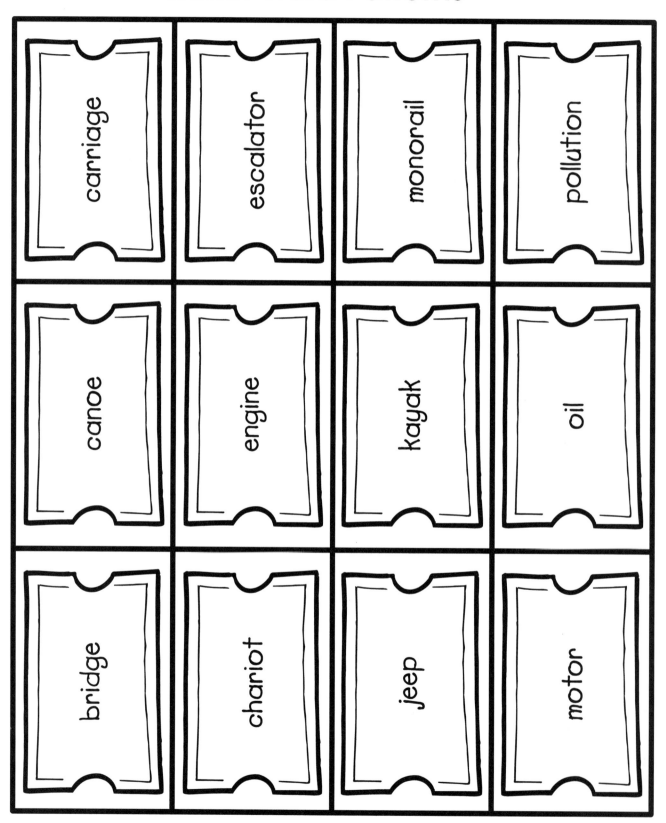

# Ticket Word Patterns

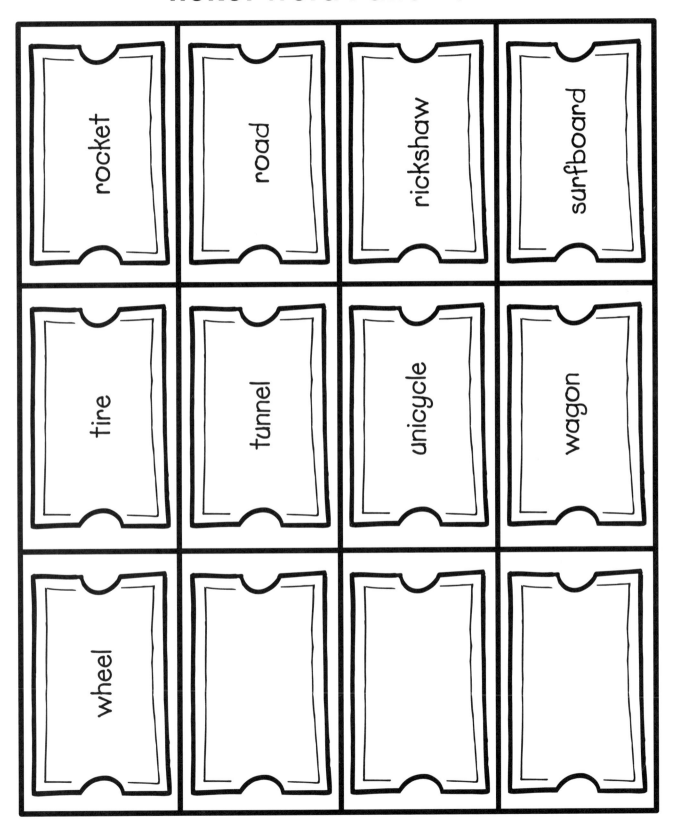

NONFICTION BOOK LINKS

# Train

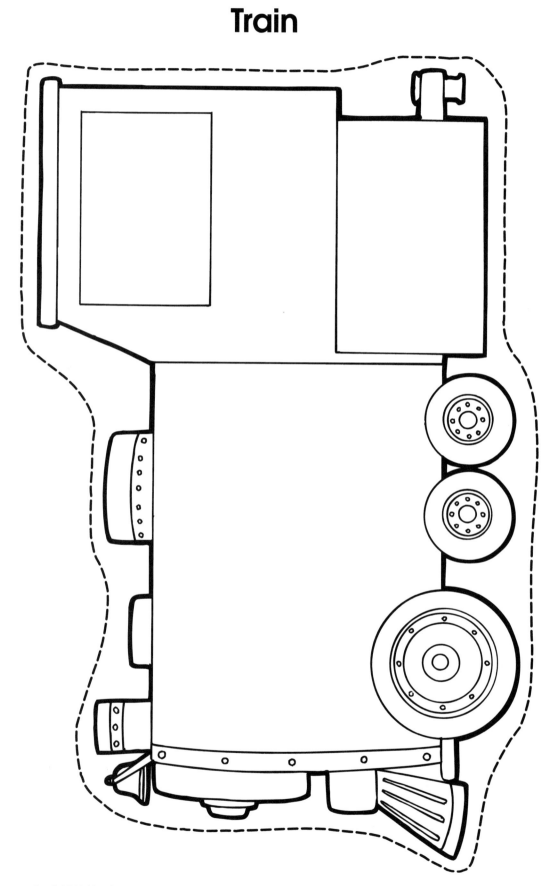

# Traffic Jam Mural

In this activity, the children will be working to create a mural of a traffic jam. Each vehicle on the mural will feature a news story about a form of transportation.

**Materials:**
"Traffic Jam" Hands-on Handout (p. 48), Automobile Pattern (p. 16), "Super-Duper Fact Cards" (p. 70-77), crayons or markers, scissors, glue, tempera paint, paintbrushes, shallow tins (for paint), butcher paper

**Directions:**
1. Duplicate a copy of the "Traffic Jam" Hands-on Handout for each child.
2. Have each child choose a form of road transportation to write about, such as a car, bus, truck, taxi, motorcycle, fire engine, or SUV.
3. The children can use the "Super-Duper Fact Cards," books, encyclopedias, or the Web to research their reports.
4. Have the children copy their reports onto the automobile patterns. Or let the children cut out their own vehicle shapes.
5. Have the class work together to create a traffic jam mural. They can paint a backdrop onto a sheet of butcher paper, then post their vehicles in a traffic jam sequence. Traffic lights can also be added.

**Option:**
• Invite a speaker to the class to discuss transportation, such as a school bus driver, race car driver, crossing guard, or police officer.

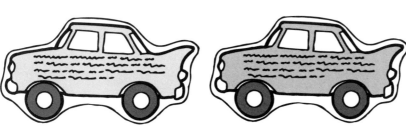

*Terrific Transportation* © 2000 Monday Morning Books, Inc.

HANDS-ON HANDOUT: SUPER-DUPER PROJECT

# Traffic Jam

**What You Do:**

1. Choose a vehicle to research, such as a car, bus, trolley, car, truck, taxi, motorcycle, or SUV. Write the name of your vehicle here:

_____

2. Research your vehicle and write down three facts about it.

_____
_____
_____

3. Brainstorm what you want to write about. For example, you could focus on how your vehicle was invented or whether it was a successful invention. (Do people still use it today?)

_____
_____
_____

4. Write a short news story about your vehicle. First, write a draft. Then copy the story onto the automobile pattern, or make your own pattern.

Terrific Transportation © 2000 Monday Morning Books, Inc.

FICTION BOOK LINKS

# The Boxcar Children

### Story:
*The Boxcar Children* by Gertrude Chandler Warner, illustrated by L. Kate Deal (Albert Whitman, 1942).
Four orphaned siblings, two boys and two girls, live together in an abandoned boxcar in the forest. They sleep in the boxcar, pick berries in the forest, and wash in a nearby brook.

### Setting the Stage:
• Display the railroad train cars (p. 19) around the room. To create a forest setting, cut out paper trees to place behind the cars.
• Serve blueberries and milk or brown bread and cheese for a snack. The students can pretend to be the children in *The Boxcar Children*.
• Have a foot race. All of the children should participate, and they should run it for fun, just like Henry.
• The four Boxcar Children go to the dump to find useful items others have discarded. Your class can set up a recycling awareness day, or a recycling center, in your school.

### Other Books in the Series:
There are 19 books in the series, including several with transportation-themes: *Bus Station Mystery*, *Caboose Mystery*, *Houseboat Mystery*, and *Bicycle Mystery*.

### Tongue Twister:
*Benny bought blue blocks, brown socks, and round rocks.*

Terrific Transportation © 2000 Monday Morning Books, Inc.

FICTION BOOK LINKS

# Write It on a Boxcar

Use *The Boxcar Children* to inspire children to write their own train-related stories. Before doing this activity, consider reading other books about trains to the children or showing them pictures in books. If you live near a Train Museum, you might take the children on a field trip.

## Materials:
Boxcar pattern (p. 51), "Super-Duper Fact Card" on trains (p. 76), pens or pencils

## Directions:
1. Explain that the children will be writing stories about trains. Children who have ridden on trains can write about their experiences. Other children might write about seeing a train go by. They can use the "Super-Duper Fact Card" on trains to spark ideas.
2. Duplicate a copy of the Boxcar pattern for each child.
3. Have the children write their stories on the boxcars.
4. Post the completed boxcar stories in a row around the classroom, or bind them together in a class book. If you post them, use the Train engine (p. 46) as a lead pattern.

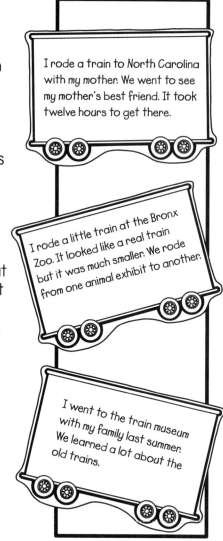

Terrific Transportation © 2000 Monday Morning Books, Inc.

FICTION BOOK LINKS

# Boxcar

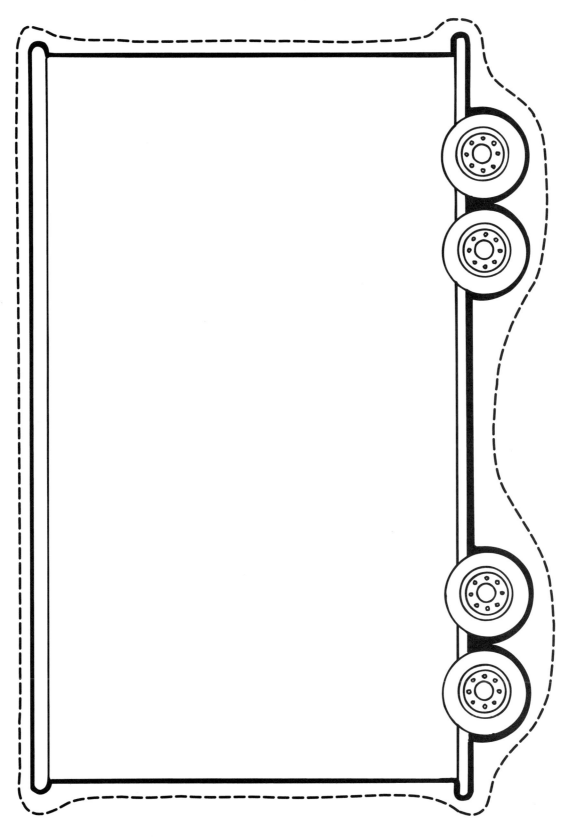

Terrific Transportation © 2000 Monday Morning Books, Inc.

FICTION BOOK LINKS

# Little House on the Prairie

### Story:
*Little House on the Prairie* by Laura Ingalls Wilder, illustrated by Garth Williams (Harper & Row, 1935). Ma, Pa, Mary, Laura, and Baby Carrie all move west from their little house in the big woods. They travel in a covered wagon, first crossing the frozen Mississippi River, and then crossing many other creeks and rivers, including the Missouri River. Laura gets to see many new creatures and objects, although she does get bored with the same landscape day after day. At night, the stars seem so close that she wishes her father could take the largest one from the sky and give it to her.

### Setting the Stage:
- Use the Prairie Schooner pattern (p. 35) to create a bulletin board display. Add crepe paper or construction paper grass around the schooners.
- Cut pictures of horses from magazines, or duplicate them from resource books, and add them to the front of the prairie schooners. Write the names Patty and Pet on the horses—these are the names of the western mustangs in *Little House on the Prairie*.
- Set out an assortment of prairie-themed books (see **Transportation Resources**) for the children to look at during free time.

### Tongue Twister:
*She slept sooner on a schooner.*

Terrific Transportation © 2000 Monday Morning Books, Inc.

FICTION BOOK LINKS

# Little House Diary

In this activity, the children will pretend to have traveled out west in a covered wagon. They will keep track of their journeys in a diary.

**Materials:**
"My Diary" pattern (p. 54), Prairie Schooner (p. 35), pens or pencils, crayons or markers, hole punch, yarn or brads

**Directions:**
1. Duplicate a copy of the diary pattern for each child.
2. Explain that the children will be writing diary entries about their imaginary journeys in covered wagons.
3. The children can illustrate their entries using crayons and markers.
4. Bind all of the diary entries in a class book. Use one of the Prairie Schooner patterns for the front cover.

**Option:**
• Consider making this an ongoing activity. Each time you read a chapter to the children, they can make a separate diary entry. Duplicate a copy of the diary pattern for each entry, or let the children write their entries on notebook paper.

Terrific Transportation © 2000 Monday Morning Books, Inc.

# My Diary

FICTION BOOK LINKS

# The Magic School Bus

### Story:
*The Magic School Bus: Lost in the Solar System* by Joanna Cole, illustrated by Bruce Degen (Scholastic, 1990).
When the planetarium is closed for repairs, a wonderfully wacky teacher named Ms. Frizzle takes her students on a wild field trip through the solar system. In their magic school bus, they visit the moon, the sun, each planet, and the asteroid belt, learning facts about the different objects along the way. An obnoxious guest student ends up saving the day after Ms. Frizzle is left behind at the asteroid belt.

### Setting the Stage:
• Cut school buses (p. 56) from yellow construction paper and post them around the room.
• Cut construction paper planets, a moon, sun, and asteroids to post around the yellow school buses.
• Show one of the videos based on the books in this series.
• Check out an assortment of the books in this series and keep them available for the children to look at on their own.

### Other Books in the Series:
Other books in this popular series include *The Magic School Bus Inside the Earth*, *The Magic School Bus at the Waterworks*, and *The Magic School Bus Inside the Human Body*.

**Note:** Choose any of the books in this series for the activity.

### Tongue Twister:
*Bring a blanket on the blue bus.*

Terrific Transportation © 2000 Monday Morning Books, Inc.

FICTION BOOK LINKS

# School Bus

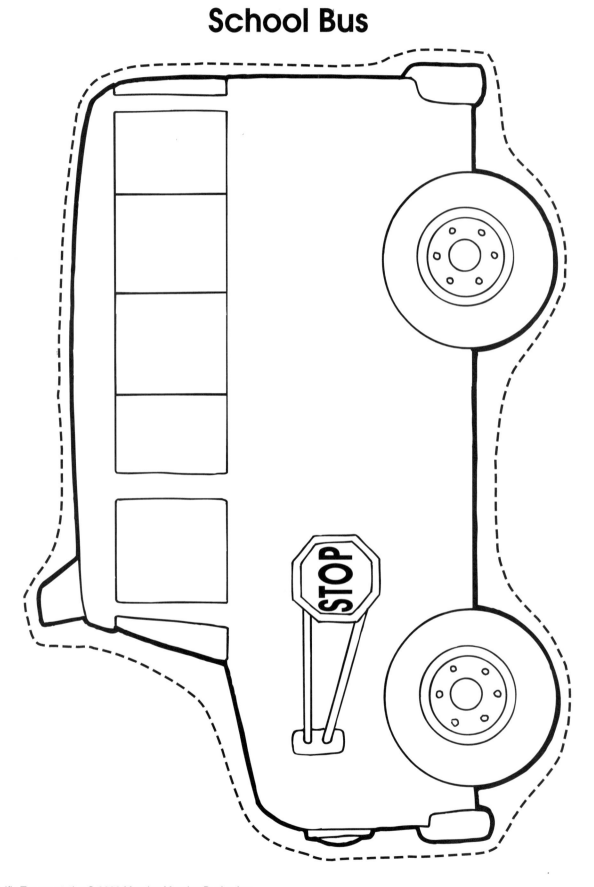

Terrific Transportation © 2000 Monday Morning Books, Inc.

FICTION BOOK LINKS

# The Magic Trailer

Children will get to stretch their imaginations, as they add magic to average trucks, helicopters, motorcycles, trailers, cars, or other forms of transportation.

## Materials:
Paper, pens or pencils, crayons or markers

## Directions:
1. Have the children each choose a form of transportation that they particularly like. They can pick a type of transportation they know well, or one that they simply think is interesting. They can choose from the Transportation A to Z List, or come up with a vehicle on their own.
2. Explain that the children will be writing stories about magic versions of their chosen forms of transportation. They will imagine that they take a trip on a magic motorcycle, or whatever their choice is, and then write a short story about the trip.
3. Children can choose to set their stories in unusual locations, in the manner of the Magic School Bus series. Or they can picture their magic form of transportation in everyday settings.
4. Have the children illustrate their completed stories. Then let them share their stories with the class.

Terrific Transportation © 2000 Monday Morning Books, Inc.

FICTION BOOK LINKS

# Chitty-Chitty-Bang-Bang

## Story:
*Chitty-Chitty-Bang-Bang: The Magical Car* by Ian Fleming, illustrated by John Burningham (Random House, 1964). The Pott family's car is full of surprises. First, when it starts, it makes a noise that sounds like chitty-chitty-bang-bang. The horn lets out a sound like Ga-goooo-ga! Even more unusual is the fact that Chitty-Chitty-Bang-Bang can fly, using her powers to get out of a horrible traffic jam. The magic car whisks the Pott family from England to the south of France. When the children stumble onto the lair of an infamous gangster, Chitty-Chitty-Bang-Bang saves the day.

## Setting the Stage:
• This book takes place in England and France. Post maps of these countries in the room for the children to see.
• Bring in British coins for the children to observe.
• Cut out pictures of cars from magazines. Add paper wings and post them around the room.
• Consider showing the video of the movie *Chitty-Chitty-Bang-Bang* staring Dick Van Dyke. (Screen the movie ahead of time yourself to determine if it is age-appropriate for your students.)

## Tongue Twister:
*A fragile magical car.*

Terrific Transportation © 2000 Monday Morning Books, Inc.

FICTION BOOK LINKS

# Chitty-Chitty for Sale

### Materials:
Drawing and writing paper, crayons or markers, pens or pencils

### Directions:
1. After you read *Chitty-Chitty-Bang-Bang*, have the children imagine that they have their own magic car.
2. Show the children pictures of Chitty-Chitty-Bang-Bang from the book. Then have them draw pictures of their own imaginary magic cars.
3. Have the children name their cars based on what their cars sound like, or what their cars can do.
4. Have the children imagine that they have to sell their cars. Each child should write a very brief advertisement describing the magical powers that their cars possess.
5. Post the pictures and the advertisements on a bulletin board where other classes, teachers, or parents can peruse the magic cars for sale.

### Option:
• Bring in the car advertisements from a local paper. Have the children look at the different types of abbreviations that car owners use. They can also determine how long advertisements usually are.

Terrific Transportation © 2000 Monday Morning Books, Inc.

FICTION BOOK LINKS: SUPER-DUPER PROJECT

# Making Mother Goose Rhymes

Mother Goose rhymes have been written for a wide variety of forms of transportation. However, there are no Mother Goose rhymes for modern vehicles, such as submarines, helicopters, or motorcycles. In this activity, students will write new Mother Goose Rhymes.

**Materials:**
Mother Goose Transportation Rhymes (p. 61), paper, pencils or pens, crayons or markers

**Directions:**
1. Duplicate a copy of the Mother Goose Transportation Rhymes for each child.
2. Have the children read the Mother Goose rhymes. Explain that they will be writing their own transportation rhymes.
3. The children can start by replacing words in the original rhymes with new forms of transportation. For example, in the Three Wise Men of Gotham rhyme, bowl could be replaced by boat, ship, or sub. In the Ride a Cock-Horse rhyme, the words motorcycle, Cadillac, and bus, could be substituted for cock-horse. For novice poets, their word-replacement poems do not need to rhyme.
4. The children can illustrate their new Mother Goose rhymes.

**Options:**
• Instead of naming the new rhymes Mother Goose rhymes, children can name themselves Mother or Father and then their own names, for instance, Mother Marilynn Rhymes or Father Scott Rhymes.
• Rather than substituting words, the children can write their own rhymes from scratch.

Terrific Transportation © 2000 Monday Morning Books, Inc.

HANDS-ON HANDOUT: SUPER-DUPER PROJECT

# Mother Goose Transportation Rhymes

**Balloon rhyme:**

What's the news of the day,
Good neighbor, I pray?
They say the balloon
Has gone up to the moon.

**Boat & Ship rhymes:**

Three wise men of Gotham
They went to sea in a bowl,
And if the bowl had been stronger
My song had been longer.

Little ships must keep the shore;
Larger ships they venture more.

**Pony & Horse rhymes:**

Yankee Doodle came to town,
Riding on a pony;
He stuck a feather in his cap
And called it macaroni.

Ride a cock-horse to Banbury Cross,
To see a fine lady upon a white horse.
Rings on her fingers and bells on her toes,
She shall have music wherever she goes.

**Walking rhyme:**

See-saw, sacradown,
Which is the way to London town?
One foot up and the other foot down,
That is the way to London town.

*Terrific Transportation* © 2000 Monday Morning Books, Inc.

IT'S SHOW TIME!

# Terrific Transportation Program

**Songs:**
- Would You Drive Real Far?
- A Hovercraft Glides on the Ocean
- Submarine, Submarine
- Oh, Give Me a Boat
- Oh, My Darling, Submarine
- Hovercrafts, Submarines, Paddleboats, and Planes

**Featuring:**

*Terrific Transportation* © 2000 Monday Morning Books, Inc.

# Would You Drive Real Far?

(to the tune of "Do Your Ears Hang Low?")

Would you drive real far
In a Model T Ford car?
Would the driving make you dizzy
In a car called the "Tin Lizzie"?
Would you want to take it back,
If it only came in black?
Would you drive real far?

# Cardboard Car Costume

## What You Need:

## What You Do:
1. Paint your box to look like a car. Add painted-on doors and handles. You might also want to paint on headlights, taillights, and license plates.
2. When the paint is dry, string a piece of yarn through each set of two holes on the boxes.
3. Wear your costume to sing songs about cars.

## Option:
- Make your car an "art car." Glue on a variety of artistic decorations, such as buttons or marbles or pictures cut from magazines. Be sure to give your art car a name!

# A Hovercraft Glides on the Ocean

(to the tune of "My Bonnie Lies Over the Ocean")

A hovercraft glides on the ocean.
It's raised above water by fans,
It carries both cargo and people,
And takes them right up on dry land,
    dry land.
Hovercrafts glide on the water, then slide
    on dry land, dry land.
Hovercrafts glide on the water, then slide
    on dry land.

# Submarine, Submarine

(to the tune of "Row, Row, Row Your Boat")

Would you like to live,
Underneath the sea?
Submarine, submarine, submarine, submarine,
That's the place for me!

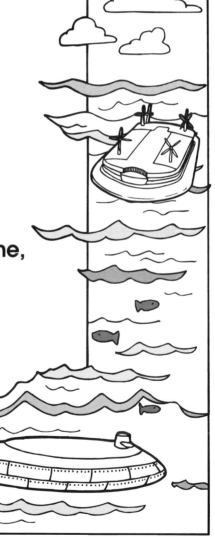

# Super Submarine Costume

## What You Need:

## What You Do:
1. Paint your box to look like a submarine. Paint on round windows.
2. When the paint is dry, string a piece of yarn through each set of two holes on the boxes.
3. Create a periscope from a bent cardboard tube. Paint it to match the submarine, then use heavy mailing tape to secure it to the box.
4. Wear the submarine costume while singing songs.

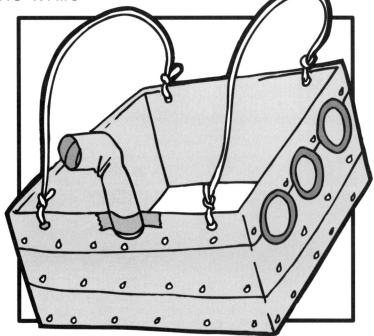

Terrific Transportation © 2000 Monday Morning Books, Inc.

# Oh, Give Me a Boat

(to the tune of "Home on the Range")

Oh, give me a boat,
So I won't sink, I'll float.
I would like to try sailing today.
I'll wait for a gale,
To put wind in my sails,
Then I'll holler out, "Anchor's Away!"

Sailing is for me,
It makes me feel happy and free.
Where the water is clear,
And there's salt in the air,
I just love to be out on the sea.

# Oh, My Darling, Submarine

(to the tune of "Clementine")

Oh, my darling,
Oh, my darling,
Oh, my darling, submarine,
Down you go,
Beneath the ocean,
In the water, blue and green.

Do you wish to see the sunshine,
Do you miss it down below?
What's it like among the sea life,
Where the jellyfishes glow?

Oh, my darling,
Oh, my darling,
Oh, my darling, submarine,
Down you go,
Beneath the ocean,
In the water, blue and green.

IT'S SHOW TIME!

# Hovercrafts, Submarines, Paddleboats, and Planes

(to the tune of "Jingle Bells")

Hovercrafts, submarines, paddleboats, and planes,
Rocket ships and sports cars, zeppelins, and trains.
They have one thing in common,
You'll guess it if you try,
They all are types of vehicles for
Water, land, and sky.

Oh, rockets fly in space,
And trains travel on rails.
Sailboats cruise the seas.
The wind fills up their sails.

Subways speed along,
Through tunnels underground.
Sports cars drive on land,
That's how we get around!

**Note:** The children can do hand motions to indicate the different types of travel each vehicle performs.

Terrific Transportation © 2000 Monday Morning Books, Inc.

SUPER-DUPER FACT CARDS

## Automobile Facts

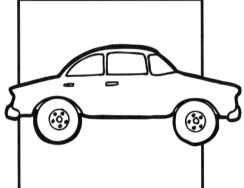

**Noisy:** The first car, built in Austria, was so noisy that police banned it.
**Early cars:** In early cars, the driver had to turn a handle on the car's front to get it started.
**Electric:** The first electric car was built in 1847.
**Modern cars:** Today's cars have many safety features that were missing from horsedrawn carriages. These include headlights, taillights, and horns.
**Super-Duper Fact:** In the future, cars will use less fuel and cause less pollution. They may be solar-powered.

## Amelia Earhart Facts

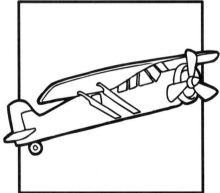

**Occupation:** Amelia Earhart was an American pilot.
**Lifetime:** Earhart lived from 1897 to 1937.
**Schooling:** Earhart studied automobile engine repair.
**Up, up, and away:** While learning, Earhart had several crash landings.
**Known for:** In 1928, Amelia Earhart became the first woman to fly across the Atlantic. In 1932, she became the first woman to fly across the Atlantic alone.
**Super-Duper Fact:** Earhart became the first person to fly alone from Hawaii to California.

Terrific Transportation © 2000 Monday Morning Books, Inc.

## Bicycle Facts

**Invented:** Bicycles were invented more than 200 years ago.
**Early cycles:** "Ordinaries" or "penny farthings" had extremely large front wheels and small rear wheels.
**Safety factor:** Tricycles, invented about 100 years ago, were safer than the ordinaries.
**1,2,3:** Tricycles have three wheels, bicycles have two, and unicycles have one.
**Bicycles built for two:** Tandems are bicycles for two riders.
**Super-Duper Fact:** Triplettes and quadruplettes carry three and four riders.

## Boat Facts

**Invented:** The first rafts were made of branches tied together.
**Dugouts:** The first real boats were made by burning or digging out the wood from inside a split tree trunk.
**Skin Boats:** Animal skins stretched over a branch or basket frame created skin boats.
**Early ships:** Ships with papyrus sails floated on the Nile in 3100 BC. Papyrus is a reedlike plant.
**Super-Duper Fact:** Around AD 850, the Vikings sailed across the Atlantic in open ships. Their ships carried 60 oarsmen on each side.

SUPER-DUPER FACT CARDS

## Henry Ford Facts

**Occupation:** Henry Ford made motor cars.
**Lifetime:** Ford lived from 1863 to 1947.
**Early Skill:** Henry could fix watches.
**Known for:** Ford designed an assembly line to make cars.
**Famous car:** Henry Ford's Model T was first sold in 1908. Nicknamed the Tin Lizzie, it could reach a top speed of 45 mph (70 kph). The assembly line made a car that ordinary people could afford.
**Super-Duper Fact:** Ford said that his car could be had in any color, so long as it was black.

## Covered Wagon Facts

**When:** Covered wagons took families across the United States.
**Mule-power:** The wagons were pulled by teams of mules or oxen.
**Traveling together:** 100 or more wagons traveled together.
**Going the Distance:** The wagons traveled about 20 miles (30 km) a day. The trip across country could take more than five months.
**Super-Duper Fact:** From a distance, covered wagons looked like sailing ships. They were nicknamed Prairie Schooners.

Terrific Transportation © 2000 Monday Morning Books, Inc.

## Hot Air Balloon Facts

**When:** The first hot-air balloon with people on board flew in 1783, in France. Australia's first hot air balloon ascent was made in 1858.
**Who:** Many balloonists were entertainers who traveled to fairs.
**How they fly:** Air expands when it is heated. A balloonful of hot air is lighter than the same volume of cold air. When the air in the balloon cools, it sinks back to the ground.
**Super-Duper Fact:** In 1250, a monk wrote a book about hollow globes that float in the air.

## Hovercraft Facts

**When:** The world's first hovercraft made its appearance in 1959.
**How:** A hovercraft rides on a cushion of high-pressure air that reduces the friction between the craft and the surface over which it travels.
**Modern developments:** Now hovercrafts can carry 220 tons (200 tonnes) of cargo for 560 miles (900 km).
**Super-Duper Fact:** In 1968, the world's largest hovercraft was created. When the hovercraft reaches its destination, it glides up a ramp onto dry land.

SUPER-DUPER FACT CARDS

## Lighthouse Facts

**When:** The world's first large lighthouse was built at Alexandria in Egypt in 250 BC.
**How big:** The first lighthouse tower stood 400 feet (120 m) high. At night, the fire burning at the top of its tower guided sailors safely into port.
**Super-Duper Fact:** In 1759, a new lighthouse was built in the English Channel. It was the first to be built with underwater-setting cement.

## Taxi Facts

**What they are:** Taxis are vehicles with drivers for hire.
**People-powered:** Not all taxis are automobiles. In the past, rickshaws were pulled by people or horses. The cycle-rickshaw is a modern, pedal-powered version. Water taxis are boat versions.
**Different colors:** In the United States, most taxis are yellow. In London, most cabs are black.
**Super-Duper Fact:** In the future, space taxis may be the way that people travel.

*Terrific Transportation* © 2000 Monday Morning Books, Inc.

## Titanic Facts

**What:** In 1912, the *Titanic* was the largest ship ever launched.
**Unsinkable:** The ship was called "unsinkable."
**Disaster:** On its first voyage, the *Titanic* hit an iceberg and sank. 1,513 people died. 2,200 people were aboard. Many of the people died because of a shortage of lifeboats.
**Good news:** Because of this disaster, safety rules for ships and an iceberg patrol were later created.
**Super-Duper Fact:** Survivors of the *Titanic* reported that the ship's orchestra played even as the ship sank.

## Tank Facts

**Description:** A military tank is an armored vehicle.
**Invented:** First used in World War I, it was developed by the British and French.
**Modern tanks:** Since World War II, the basic features of tanks have remained unchanged.
**Buggy:** The tank runs on caterpillar tracks, also called "crawler tracks." These tracks let the vehicles cross rough terrain by laying down their own metal "road."
**Super-Duper Fact:** The word "tank" was a secret code name given to the new vehicle at the end of 1915.

SUPER-DUPER FACT CARDS

## Train Facts

**Horse-power:** Early trains were pulled by horses. The first railroad locomotive was built in England in 1803.
**Fast:** By the 1850s, trains traveled at 50 mph (80 kph).
**Inexpensive:** Because rail travel was cheap, people who had never been on a trip could afford to travel by train.
**Faster:** In 1964, Japan introduced high-speed "bullet trains," capable of 130 mph (210 kph).
**Super-Duper Fact:** People worried that the first trains would go too fast for passengers to be able to breathe.

## Truck Facts

**First truck:** The first truck was built in 1769 by a Frenchman.
**Early trucks:** Early trucks were powered by steam.
**Drivers:** Truck drivers spend so many hours on the road, that often their trucks have living areas for the driver to use.
**Swimmers:** Trucks that "swim" are called "amphibious trucks." These trucks are often used by the military.
**Super-Duper Fact:** An Australian road-train was the longest truck in the world. It was as long as 15 cars and had 110 wheels!

Terrific Transportation © 2000 Monday Morning Books, Inc.

SUPER-DUPER FACT CARDS

## Wright Brothers Facts

**Jobs:** The Wright brothers owned a bicycle shop.
**Lifetime:** Orville Wright lived from 1871 to 1948. Wilbur Wright lived from 1867 to 1912.
**Known for:** The Wright brothers made the first flight in an airplane with an engine on December 17, 1908 near Kitty Hawk, North Carolina.
**Inspired by:** They probably got their idea from a man named Otto Lilienthal who made flights in gliders.
**Super-Duper Fact:** The Wright brothers' entire first flight could have taken place inside a modern jumbo jet.

## Zeppelin Facts

**Description:** A zeppelin was an airship made of stretched cloth over a frame of metal or wood.
**How it worked:** Hydrogen-filled gas bags inside the airship gave the lifting force.
**When it was used:** In 1900, Count Ferdinand von Zeppelin tried out the first of his rigid airships. His company built more than 100 "zeppelins" over the next 30 years.
**Super-Duper Fact:** Zeppelins could be up to 650 feet (200 m) long.

Terrific Transportation © 2000 Monday Morning Books, Inc.

# Transportation A to Z List

**A:** Airplane, Airport, Automobile
**B:** Balloon, Bicycle
**C:** Cable Car, Canoe, Car, Caravan, Cruise Ship
**D:** Diesel Engine
**E:** Elevator, Escalator
**F:** Fire Engine
**G:** Gasoline, Gearbox, Gondola
**H:** Helicopter
**I:** Ice Skates
**J:** Jeep
**K:** Kayak
**L:** Lifeboat, Locomotive
**M:** Monoplane, Motorcycle
**N:** Nuclear Submarine
**O:** Oil, *Orient Express*
**P:** Paddleboat, Pony Express
**Q:** Quffa (basket-boats from Babylonia)
**R:** Raft, Railroad, Riverboat
**S:** Sails, Scooter, Seat Belt, Space Shuttle
**T:** Tank, Traffic Lights, Train, Truck
**U:** U-Boat
**V:** Vespa Scooter, *Voyager* aircraft
**W:** Wagon, Warship, Wheelbarrow
**X:** X-15A-2 aircraft (research aircraft circa 1967)
**Y:** Yoke
**Z:** Zeppelin

# Transportation Resources

### Automobiles:
- *Car* by Richard Sutton (Knopf, 1990).
- *Cars and Trucks* by Philip Steele (Crestwood House, 1991).
- *Cars and How They Work* by Gordon Cruikshank, illustrated by Alan Austin (Dorling Kindersley, 1992).

### Bicycles:
- *The Bicycle & How It Works* by David Inglis Urquhart (Henry Z. Walck, 1972).
- *Bicycle Book* by Gail Gibbons (Holiday House, 1995).

### Covered Wagons:
- *Caddie Woodlawn* by Carol Ryrie Brink (Macmillan, 1935). A Newbery Award winner.
- *The Cowboy Trade* by Glen Rounds (Holiday House, 1972).
- *Grandma Essie's Covered Wagon* by David Williams, illustrated by Wiktor Sadowski (Knopf, 1993).
- *Sarah, Plain and Tall* by Patricia MacLachlan (Harper & Row, 1985).
- *The Way West* by Amelia Stewart Knight (Simon & Schuster, 1993).

### Earhart, Amelia:
- *A Picture Book of Amelia Earhart* by David A. Adler, illustrated by Jeff Fisher (Holiday House, 1998). This is a perfect book for beginning researchers.

### Ford, Henry:
*Wheels of Time: A Biography of Henry Ford* by Catherine Gourley, in association with Henry Ford Museum & Greenfield Village (Millbrook, 1997).

### Lighthouses:
- *Beacons of Light: Lighthouses* by Gail Gibbons (Morrow, 1990).
- *Lighthouses: Watchers at Sea* by Brenda Z. Guiberson (Henry Holt, 1995).

### Motorcycle:
- *The Mouse and the Motorcycle* by Beverly Cleary (Yearling, 1965). This is a chapter book by the author of the *Ramona* series.

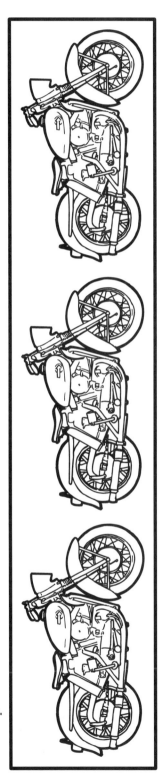

RESOURCES

# Transportation Resources

### Pony Express:
• *Pony Express!* by Steven Kroll, illustrated by Dan Andreasen (Scholastic, 1996).

### Titanic:
• *Exploring the Titanic* by Robert D. Ballard (Scholastic, 1988).
• *On Board the Titanic* by Shelley Tanaka (Hyperion, 1996).
• *The Titanic Lost-and-Found* by Judy Donnelly (Random House, 1987).

### Trains:
• *The Freight Train Book* by Jack Pierce (Carolrhoda, 1980).
• *Trains at Work* by Richard Ammon, photographs by Darrell Peterson and Richard Ammon (Atheneum, 1993).

### Wright Brothers:
• *The Wright Brothers* by Charles Graves, illustrated by Fermin Rocker (Putnam's, 1973).

### Transportation-themed Game:
• Battleship

### Transportation-themed Stickers:
Stickers featuring vehicles, street signs, hot air balloons, etc. are available from Mrs. Grossman's.

### Transportation Web Sites:
Henry Ford site:
http://www.modelt.org/kidintro.html

Hot air balloon site:
http://www.pbs.org/wgbh/nova/balloon/virtual/virtual01.html

*Terrific Transportation* © 2000 Monday Morning Books, Inc.